D1325974

LITERARY
WIT &
WISDOM

Quips and Quotes to Suit
All Manner of Occasions

RICHARD BENSON

LITERARY WIT AND WISDOM

Summersdale Publishers Ltd
46 West Street
Chichester
West Sussex
PO19 1RP
UK

www.summersdale.com

Printed and bound in the Czech Republic

ISBN: 978-1-84953-840-4

Substantial discounts on bulk quantities of Summersdale books are available to corporations, professional associations and other organisations. For details contact Nicky Douglas by telephone: +44 (0) 1243 756902, fax: +44 (0) 1243 786300 or email: nicky@summersdale.com.

CONTENTS

EDITOR'S NOTE

Books are little universes that we hold in our hands. Some are eerily similar to our own, so much so that they appear to be telling our own lives back to us, with only a sunset altered here or a new friend there. Some are wild and strange to us, filled with Amazonian warriors astride unfamiliar beasts and spaceships no bigger than our thumbnail. Some speak to us in sparse, elegant prose and verse, shorn of everything but the best words in the best order. Others fizz with the sheer ecstasy of language, bursting with words that pop and slither and hum. All contain truth.

These truths are beautiful, but just as often sharp and witty, with authors laughing as much at themselves as they do at the reader. After all, as Samuel Johnson said, 'No man but a blockhead ever wrote, except for money.' Indeed, sometimes they turn the knife on each other, as when Mark Twain observes 'I go as far as to say that any library is a good library that does not contain a volume by Jane Austen. Even if it contains no other book.' For every instance of stinging wit there can be found phrases of hope and joy: Eleanor Farjeon reminds us that 'Love has no uttermost, as the stars have no number and the sea no rest.'

These memorable quotes, and many more, can be found in this collection of literary wit and wisdom.

WRITES
AND
WRONGS

There are three rules for writing
the novel. Unfortunately, no
one knows what they are.

W. SOMERSET MAUGHAM

A GOOD NOVEL TELLS US THE
TRUTH ABOUT ITS HERO; BUT
A BAD NOVEL TELLS US THE
TRUTH ABOUT ITS AUTHOR.

G. K. CHESTERTON

When you catch an adjective, kill it.

MARK TWAIN

WHAT IS WRITTEN WITHOUT
EFFORT IS IN GENERAL READ
WITHOUT PLEASURE.

SAMUEL JOHNSON

Unprovided with original learning,
unformed in the habits of thinking,
unskilled in the arts of composition,
I resolved to write a book.

EDWARD GIBBON

WRITING IS LIKE GETTING
MARRIED. ONE SHOULD NEVER
COMMIT ONESELF UNTIL ONE
IS AMAZED AT ONE'S LUCK.

IRIS MURDOCH

I can't understand these chaps who go round American universities explaining how they write poems; it's like going round explaining how you sleep with your wife.

PHILIP LARKIN

WRITING TODAY IS LIKE STANDING STARK NAKED IN TRAFALGAR SQUARE AND BEING TOLD TO GET AN ERECTION.

LOUIS DE BERNIÈRES

I was working on the proof of one of my poems all the morning, and took out a comma. In the afternoon I put it back again.

OSCAR WILDE

The most essential gift for a good writer is a built-in, shockproof, shit-detector.

ERNEST HEMINGWAY

Literature is mostly about having sex and not much about having children. Life is the other way round.

DAVID LODGE

A SEQUEL IS AN ADMISSION
THAT YOU'VE BEEN REDUCED
TO IMITATING YOURSELF.

DON MARQUIS

We write to taste life twice, in
the moment and in retrospect.

ANAÏS NIN

YOU NEVER HAVE TO
CHANGE ANYTHING YOU
GOT UP IN THE MIDDLE OF
THE NIGHT TO WRITE.

SAUL BELLOW

Substitute 'damn' every time you're inclined to write 'very'; your editor will delete it and the writing will be just as it should be.

MARK TWAIN

THE ROAD TO HELL IS PAVED WITH ADVERBS.

STEPHEN KING

A man's got to take a lot of punishment to write a really funny book.

ERNEST HEMINGWAY

DON'T TELL ME THE MOON IS
SHINING; SHOW ME THE GLINT
OF LIGHT ON BROKEN GLASS.

ANTON CHEKHOV

How vain it is to sit down to write
when you have not stood up to live!

HENRY DAVID THOREAU

NO MAN BUT A
BLOCKHEAD EVER WROTE,
EXCEPT FOR MONEY.

SAMUEL JOHNSON

Nothing that happens to a
writer – however happy, however
tragic – is ever wasted.

P. D. JAMES

EASY READING IS DAMN
HARD WRITING.

NATHANIEL HAWTHORNE

Writing is easy. All you do is stare at a blank sheet of paper until drops of blood form on your forehead.

GENE FOWLER

STORY OF

MY LIFE

Life is rather like opening a
tin of sardines – we're all of
us looking for the key.

ALAN BENNETT

IT IS DANGEROUS TO BE
SINCERE UNLESS YOU
ARE ALSO STUPID.

GEORGE BERNARD SHAW

Men must live and create.
Live to the point of tears.

ALBERT CAMUS

FOR WHAT DO WE LIVE, BUT TO MAKE SPORT FOR OUR NEIGHBOURS, AND LAUGH AT THEM IN OUR TURN?

JANE AUSTEN

Life is a gamble at terrible odds – if it was a bet, you wouldn't take it.

TOM STOPPARD

MY LIFE LOOKED GOOD ON PAPER – WHERE, IN FACT, ALMOST ALL OF IT WAS BEING LIVED.

MARTIN AMIS

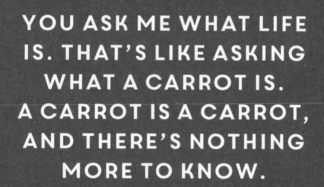

YOU ASK ME WHAT LIFE
IS. THAT'S LIKE ASKING
WHAT A CARROT IS.
A CARROT IS A CARROT,
AND THERE'S NOTHING
MORE TO KNOW.

Anton Chekhov

You fall out of your mother's womb, you crawl across open country under fire, and drop into your grave.

QUENTIN CRISP

THE MEANING OF LIFE IS THAT IT STOPS.

FRANZ KAFKA

Life is one long process of getting tired.

SAMUEL BUTLER

THOUGH A GOOD DEAL IS
TOO STRANGE TO BE BELIEVED,
NOTHING IS TOO STRANGE
TO HAVE HAPPENED.

THOMAS HARDY

In three words I can sum
up everything I've learned
about life: it goes on.

ROBERT FROST

TO TRAVEL HOPEFULLY
IS A BETTER THING
THAN TO ARRIVE.

ROBERT LOUIS STEVENSON

When we are born, we
cry that we are come
To this great stage of fools.

WILLIAM SHAKESPEARE

TO LIVE IS THE RAREST
THING IN THE WORLD. MOST
PEOPLE EXIST, THAT IS ALL.

GEORGE ORWELL

I want to live and feel all the shades,
tones and variations of mental and
physical experience possible.

SYLVIA PLATH

I LOVE SHERLOCK HOLMES.
MY LIFE IS SO UNTIDY
AND HE'S SO NEAT.

DOROTHY PARKER

May you live all the
days of your life.

JONATHAN SWIFT

LIFE'S A BITCH. YOU'VE GOT
TO GO OUT AND KICK ASS.

MAYA ANGELOU

IF I CAN STOP ONE
HEART FROM BREAKING,
I SHALL NOT LIVE
IN VAIN.

Emily Dickinson

It is said that your life flashes before your eyes just before you die. That is true, it's called Life.

TERRY PRATCHETT

A WOMAN HAS TO LIVE HER LIFE, OR LIVE TO REPENT NOT HAVING LIVED IT.

D. H. LAWRENCE

Unbeing dead isn't being alive.

E. E. CUMMINGS

AUTHORS ON
THE ARTS

ALL ART IS
QUITE USELESS.

OSCAR WILDE

There are only two styles of portrait
painting; the serious and the smirk.

CHARLES DICKENS

THERE ARE TWO MEN
INSIDE THE ARTIST, THE
POET AND THE CRAFTSMAN.
ONE IS BORN A POET. ONE
BECOMES A CRAFTSMAN.

ÉMILE ZOLA

Art, like morality, consists of drawing the line somewhere.

G. K. CHESTERTON

I DOUBT THAT ART NEEDED RUSKIN ANY MORE THAN A MOVING TRAIN NEEDS ONE OF ITS PASSENGERS TO SHOVE IT.

TOM STOPPARD

Nothing is capable of being well set to music that is not nonsense.

JOSEPH ADDISON

IN ART, THE BEST IS
GOOD ENOUGH.

JOHANN WOLFGANG VON GOETHE

Good painters imitate nature,
bad ones spew it up.

MIGUEL DE CERVANTES

ART IS A
JEALOUS MISTRESS.

RALPH WALDO EMERSON

The man that hath no
music in himself,
Nor is not moved with
concord of sweet sounds,
Is fit for treasons,
stratagems, and spoils.

WILLIAM SHAKESPEARE

THE HISTORY OF ART IS THE HISTORY OF REVIVALS.

SAMUEL BUTLER

There is no more sombre enemy of
good art than the pram in the hall.

CYRIL CONNOLLY

The air of ideas is the only air worth breathing.

EDITH WHARTON

[The mirror] is a symbol of Irish art. The cracked looking-glass of a servant.

JAMES JOYCE

THERE IS ONLY ONE POSITION
FOR AN ARTIST ANYWHERE:
AND THAT IS, UPRIGHT.

DYLAN THOMAS

Portrait painters tend to regard
faces as not very still lives.

ALAN BENNETT

SELF-CONSCIOUSNESS IS THE
ENEMY OF ALL ART, BE IT
ACTING, WRITING, PAINTING,
OR LIVING ITSELF, WHICH IS
THE GREATEST ART OF ALL.

RAY BRADBURY

Hell is full of musical amateurs: music is the brandy of the damned.

GEORGE BERNARD SHAW

There is no such thing as a moral
or an immoral book. Books are well
written, or badly written. That is all.

OSCAR WILDE

THE ARTIST IS NOTHING
WITHOUT THE GIFT, BUT
THE GIFT IS NOTHING
WITHOUT WORK.

ÉMILE ZOLA

Treat a work of art like a prince.
Let it speak to you first.

ARTHUR SCHOPENHAUER

GATHER YE
ROSEBUDS

THE WISE WRITER... WRITES
FOR THE YOUTH OF HIS
OWN GENERATION.

F. SCOTT FITZGERALD

Youth is wasted on the young.

CAMILLE PAGLIA

IT MUST BE WONDERFUL
TO BE 17, AND TO KNOW
EVERYTHING.

ARTHUR C. CLARKE

There is no sinner like a
young saint.

APHRA BEHN

I THOUGHT I HATED
EVERYBODY, BUT WHEN I GREW
UP I REALISED IT WAS JUST
CHILDREN I DIDN'T LIKE.

PHILIP LARKIN

If from infancy you treat children
as gods, they are liable in
adulthood to act as devils.

P. D. JAMES

YOUTH IS HAPPY BECAUSE
IT HAS THE CAPACITY TO
SEE BEAUTY. ANYONE WHO
KEEPS THE ABILITY TO SEE
BEAUTY NEVER GROWS OLD.

FRANZ KAFKA

Be on the alert to recognise
your prime at whatever time
of your life it may occur.

MURIEL SPARK

WHAT IS YOUTH EXCEPT A
MAN OR A WOMAN BEFORE IT
IS READY OR FIT TO BE SEEN?

EVELYN WAUGH

What Youth deemed crystal,
Age finds out was dew.

ROBERT BROWNING

AGE MAY HAVE ONE SIDE,
BUT ASSUREDLY YOUTH
HAS THE OTHER. THERE IS
NOTHING MORE CERTAIN
THAN THAT BOTH ARE
RIGHT, EXCEPT PERHAPS
THAT BOTH ARE WRONG.

ROBERT BURNS

The surest way to corrupt a youth
is to instruct him to hold in higher
esteem those who think alike than
those who think differently.

FRIEDRICH NIETZSCHE

YOUTH SMILES WITHOUT ANY REASON. IT IS ONE OF ITS CHIEFEST CHARMS.

Oscar Wilde

IT IS VERY DIFFICULT TO
TELL THE TRUTH, AND
YOUNG PEOPLE ARE
RARELY CAPABLE OF IT.

LEO TOLSTOY

If you're young and talented,
it's like you have wings.

HARUKI MURAKAMI

THE YOUNG HAVE ASPIRATIONS
THAT NEVER COME TO PASS,
THE OLD HAVE REMINISCENCES
OF WHAT NEVER HAPPENED.

SAKI

One does not expect old
heads on young shoulders.

C. S. LEWIS

NO MAN KNOWS HE IS YOUNG
WHILE HE IS YOUNG.

G. K. CHESTERTON

Everybody's youth is a dream,
a form of chemical madness.

F. SCOTT FITZGERALD

THE CHILDHOOD SHOWS THE MAN, AS MORNING SHOWS THE DAY.

JOHN MILTON

Youth is wholly experimental.

ROBERT LOUIS STEVENSON

ALL'S WELL THAT FRIENDS WELL

EACH FRIEND REPRESENTS
A WORLD IN US, A WORLD
POSSIBLY NOT BORN
UNTIL THEY ARRIVE.

ANAÏS NIN

Incessant company is as bad
as solitary confinement.

VIRGINIA WOOLF

HE'S MY FRIEND THAT SPEAKS
WELL OF ME BEHIND MY BACK.

THOMAS FULLER

Thy friendship oft has made
my heart to ache:
Do be my enemy – for
friendship's sake.

WILLIAM BLAKE

WE MAKE OUR FRIENDS,
WE MAKE OUR ENEMIES;
BUT GOD MAKES OUR
NEXT-DOOR NEIGHBOUR.

G. K. CHESTERTON

Friendship is a sheltering tree.

SAMUEL TAYLOR COLERIDGE

WHAT DRAWS PEOPLE TO BE FRIENDS IS THAT THEY SEE THE SAME TRUTH. THEY SHARE IT.

C. S. LEWIS

There is nothing I would not do for those who are really my friends.

JANE AUSTEN

'TIS THE PRIVILEGE OF FRIENDSHIP TO TALK NONSENSE, AND TO HAVE HER NONSENSE RESPECTED.

CHARLES LAMB

A friend is someone who knows all about you and still loves you.

ELBERT HUBBARD

In prosperity, our friends know us; in adversity, we know our friends.

JOHN CHURTON COLLINS

It is one of the blessings of
old friends that you can afford
to be stupid with them.

RALPH WALDO EMERSON

I CHOOSE MY FRIENDS
FOR THEIR GOOD LOOKS,
MY ACQUAINTANCES FOR
THEIR GOOD CHARACTERS,
AND MY ENEMIES FOR
THEIR GOOD INTELLECTS.

OSCAR WILDE

Love is blind; friendship
closes its eyes.

FRIEDRICH NIETZSCHE

A FRIEND IS ONE TO WHOM
ONE MAY POUR OUT THE
CONTENTS OF ONE'S HEART,
CHAFF AND GRAIN TOGETHER,
KNOWING THAT GENTLE
HANDS WILL TAKE AND SIFT IT.

GEORGE ELIOT

You know a real friend? Someone
you know will look after your
cat after you are gone.

WILLIAM S. BURROUGHS

I HAVE NO TALENT FOR
MAKING NEW FRIENDS,
BUT OH SUCH GENIUS FOR
FIDELITY TO OLD ONES.

DAPHNE DU MAURIER

Good friends, good books, and a sleepy conscience: this is the ideal life.

MARK TWAIN

We English are good at forgiving
our enemies; it releases us from the
obligation of liking our friends.

P. D. JAMES

WHEN A SINISTER PERSON
MEANS TO BE YOUR
ENEMY, THEY ALWAYS
START BY TRYING TO
BECOME YOUR FRIEND.

WILLIAM BLAKE

Some people go to priests; others
to poetry; I to my friends.

VIRGINIA WOOLF

IT'S ALL
RELATIVE

A FAMILY IS A TYRANNY
RULED OVER BY ITS
WEAKEST MEMBER.

GEORGE BERNARD SHAW

Familiarity breeds contempt
– and children.

MARK TWAIN

AFTER A GOOD DINNER ONE
CAN FORGIVE ANYBODY,
EVEN ONE'S OWN RELATIONS.

OSCAR WILDE

Important families are like potatoes.
The best parts are underground.

FRANCIS BACON

DON'T HOLD YOUR PARENTS
UP TO CONTEMPT. AFTER ALL...
IT IS JUST POSSIBLE THAT YOU
MAY TAKE AFTER THEM.

EVELYN WAUGH

War... panders to instincts
already well catered for within
the scope of any respectable
domestic establishment.

ALAN BENNETT

IT IS A MELANCHOLY TRUTH
THAT EVEN GREAT MEN HAVE
THEIR POOR RELATIONS.

CHARLES DICKENS

All happy families resemble one
another, but each unhappy family
is unhappy in its own way.

LEO TOLSTOY

IF YOU CANNOT GET RID OF
THE FAMILY SKELETON, YOU
MAY AS WELL MAKE IT DANCE.

GEORGE BERNARD SHAW

This was the trouble with
families. Like invidious doctors,
they knew just where it hurt.

ARUNDHATI ROY

IF A MAN'S CHARACTER IS TO
BE ABUSED, SAY WHAT YOU
WILL, THERE'S NOBODY LIKE A
RELATION TO DO THE BUSINESS.

WILLIAM MAKEPEACE THACKERAY

The place of the father in the modern
suburban family is a very small
one, particularly if he plays golf.

BERTRAND RUSSELL

FEW MISFORTUNES CAN
BEFALL A BOY WHICH BRING
WORSE CONSEQUENCES
THAN TO HAVE A REALLY
AFFECTIONATE MOTHER.

W. SOMERSET MAUGHAM

There is no friend like a sister
in calm or stormy weather.

CHRISTINA ROSSETTI

FAMILIES BREAK UP WHEN
PEOPLE TAKE HINTS YOU
DON'T INTEND AND MISS
HINTS YOU DO INTEND.

ROBERT FROST

A LADY, WITHOUT A FAMILY, WAS THE VERY BEST PRESERVER OF FURNITURE IN THE WORLD.

Jane Austen

Our own front door can be a wonderful thing, or a sight we dread; rarely is it only a door.

JEANETTE WINTERSON

ACCIDENTS WILL OCCUR IN THE BEST-REGULATED FAMILIES.

CHARLES DICKENS

It is a wise child that knows its own father, and an unusual one that unreservedly approves of him.

MARK TWAIN

STICKS
AND
STONES

THERE ARE TWO WAYS OF DISLIKING POETRY, ONE WAY IS TO DISLIKE IT, THE OTHER IS TO READ POPE.

OSCAR WILDE

We were put to Dickens as children but it never quite took. That unremitting humanity soon had me cheesed off.

ALAN BENNETT

WE ALL HAVE NAMES WE DON'T KNOW ABOUT AND DON'T WANT TO HEAR.

MARTIN AMIS

Sir, I have found you an argument;
but I am not obliged to find
you an understanding.

SAMUEL JOHNSON

HE IS MORALLY INSENSITIVE AND AESTHETICALLY DISGUSTING.

GEORGE ORWELL ON RUDYARD KIPLING

The work of a queasy undergraduate
scratching his pimples.

VIRGINIA WOOLF ON *ULYSSES* BY JAMES JOYCE

HE OWES HIS CELEBRITY MERELY TO HIS ANTIQUITY.

LORD BYRON ON GEOFFREY CHAUCER

You look wise. Pray correct that error.

CHARLES LAMB

NO ONE CAN HAVE A HIGHER OPINION OF HIM THAN I HAVE, AND I THINK HE'S A DIRTY LITTLE BEAST.

W. S. GILBERT

You beat your pate,
and fancy wit will come:
Knock as you please,
there's nobody at home.

ALEXANDER POPE

I regard you with an
indifference closely
bordering on aversion.

ROBERT LOUIS STEVENSON

He hath never fed of the dainties that are bred in a book; he hath not eat paper, as it were; he hath not drunk ink: his intellect is not replenished.

WILLIAM SHAKESPEARE

AS A SLEUTH YOU ARE POOR. YOU COULDN'T DETECT A BASS-DRUM IN A TELEPHONE-BOOTH.

P. G. WODEHOUSE

A fly, sir, may sting a stately horse, and make him wince; but one is but an insect, and the other is a horse still.

SAMUEL JOHNSON

I love Americans, but not when they try to talk French. What a blessing it is that they never try to talk English.

SAKI

WHY DON'T YOU WRITE BOOKS PEOPLE CAN READ?

NORA BARNACLE TO HER HUSBAND JAMES JOYCE

There are books of which
the backs and covers are
by far the best parts.

CHARLES DICKENS

SOME EDITORS ARE FAILED WRITERS, BUT SO ARE MOST WRITERS.

T. S. ELIOT

I go so far as to say that any library
is a good library that does not
contain a volume by Jane Austen.
Even if it contains no other book.

MARK TWAIN

IF YOU CAN'T ANNOY
SOMEBODY WITH WHAT
YOU WRITE, I THINK THERE'S
LITTLE POINT IN WRITING.

KINGSLEY AMIS

Only dull people are
brilliant at breakfast.

OSCAR WILDE

AGE CANNOT
WITHER US
(VERY MUCH)

AT 50, EVERYONE HAS
THE FACE HE DESERVES.

GEORGE ORWELL

The older one grows, the
more one likes indecency.

VIRGINIA WOOLF

THERE IS ONLY ONE CURE FOR
GREY HAIR. IT WAS INVENTED
BY A FRENCHMAN. IT IS
CALLED THE GUILLOTINE.

P. G. WODEHOUSE

To get back my youth I would
do anything in the world,
except take exercise, get up
early, or be respectable.

OSCAR WILDE

MY SUN SETS TO
RISE AGAIN.

ROBERT BROWNING

You can be young without money
but you can't be old without it.

TENNESSEE WILLIAMS

PEOPLE ALWAYS LIVE FOREVER
WHEN THERE IS ANY
ANNUITY TO BE PAID THEM.

JANE AUSTEN

Time and tide will wait for no
man, saith the adage. But all men
have to wait for time and tide.

CHARLES DICKENS

I WASTED TIME, AND NOW
DOTH TIME WASTE ME.

WILLIAM SHAKESPEARE

The wiser mind mourns less
for what Age takes away, than
what it leaves behind.

WILLIAM WORDSWORTH

THE AFTERNOON KNOWS
WHAT THE MORNING
NEVER SUSPECTED.

ROBERT FROST

We don't stop playing because
we grow old; we grow old
because we stop playing.

GEORGE BERNARD SHAW

THE OLDER I
GROW, THE MORE I
DISTRUST THE FAMILIAR
DOCTRINE THAT AGE
BRINGS WISDOM.

H. L. Mencken

AGE DOES NOT PROTECT
YOU FROM LOVE. BUT
LOVE, TO SOME EXTENT,
PROTECTS YOU FROM AGE.

ANAÏS NIN

At 80 things do not occur;
they recur.

ALAN BENNETT

TRUE TERROR IS TO WAKE
UP ONE MORNING AND
DISCOVER THAT YOUR
HIGH SCHOOL CLASS IS
RUNNING THE COUNTRY.

KURT VONNEGUT

If this is dying, then I don't
think much of it.

LYTTON STRACHEY

WE ARE SUCH STUFF AS
DREAMS ARE MADE ON;
AND OUR LITTLE LIFE IS
ROUNDED WITH A SLEEP.

WILLIAM SHAKESPEARE

Old age comes on suddenly, and
not gradually as is thought.

EMILY DICKINSON

I DON'T BELIEVE IN AGEING.
I BELIEVE IN FOREVER
ALTERING ONE'S ASPECT
TO THE SUN.

VIRGINIA WOOLF

We are always the
same age inside.

GERTRUDE STEIN

CRIT
WITTED

HAS ANYBODY EVER SEEN
A DRAMA CRITIC IN THE
DAYTIME? I DOUBT IT.

P. G. WODEHOUSE

It's easier to write about those
you hate – just as it's easier to
criticise a bad play or a bad book.

DOROTHY PARKER

CRITICS ARE LIKE BRUSHERS
OF NOBLEMEN'S CLOTHES.

HENRY WOTTON

I never read a book before reviewing it; it prejudices a man so.

SYDNEY SMITH

A MAN MUST SERVE HIS TIME TO EV'RY TRADE SAVE CENSURE – CRITICS ALL ARE READY MADE.

LORD BYRON

A bad review may spoil your breakfast but you shouldn't allow it to spoil your lunch.

KINGSLEY AMIS

I'D RATHER BE HISSED AT
FOR A GOOD VERSE, THAN
APPLAUDED FOR A BAD ONE.

VICTOR HUGO

Criticism is a study by which men
grow important and formidable
at very small expense.

SAMUEL JOHNSON

THERE IS A SORT OF
SAVAGE NOBILITY ABOUT
HIS FIRM RELIANCE ON
HIS OWN BAD TASTE.

**A. E. HOUSMAN ON THE CLASSICAL SCHOLAR
AND CRITIC RICHARD BENTLEY**

Men over 40 are no judges of a book written in a new spirit.

RALPH WALDO EMERSON

Prolonged, indiscriminate reviewing of books is a quite exceptionally thankless, irritating and exhausting job.

GEORGE ORWELL

When I read something saying I've not done anything as good as *Catch-22* I'm tempted to reply, 'Who has?'

JOSEPH HELLER

HOW MUCH EASIER IT IS TO BE CRITICAL THAN TO BE CORRECT.

BENJAMIN DISRAELI

You need a high degree of corruption or a very big heart to love absolutely everything.

GUSTAVE FLAUBERT

*Write how you want,
the critic shall show the
world you could have
written better.*

OLIVER GOLDSMITH

A BAD REVIEW IS EVEN LESS IMPORTANT THAN WHETHER IT IS RAINING IN PATAGONIA.

IRIS MURDOCH

People who are paid to have attitudes toward things, professional critics, make me sick; camp following eunuchs of literature.

ERNEST HEMINGWAY

A LOUSE IN THE LOCKS OF LITERATURE.

ALFRED, LORD TENNYSON ON LITERARY CRITIC JOHN CHURTON COLLINS

Reviewers, with some rare exceptions, are a most stupid and malignant race. As a bankrupt thief turns thief-taker in despair, so an unsuccessful author turns critic.

PERCY BYSSHE SHELLEY

TO AVOID CRITICISM,
DO NOTHING, SAY
NOTHING, BE NOTHING.

ELBERT HUBBARD

Unless a reviewer has the courage
to give you unqualified praise,
I say ignore the bastard.

JOHN STEINBECK

GLASS HALF
EMPTY

ALWAYS BORROW MONEY FROM A PESSIMIST. HE WON'T EXPECT IT BACK.

OSCAR WILDE

Every time a friend succeeds, a little something in me dies.

GORE VIDAL

THE SOONER EVERY PARTY BREAKS UP THE BETTER.

JANE AUSTEN

If you live long enough, you'll see that every victory turns into a defeat.

SIMONE DE BEAUVOIR

NOTHING AGREES WITH ME. IF I DRINK COFFEE, IT GIVES ME DYSPEPSIA; IF I DRINK WINE, IT GIVES ME THE GOUT; IF I GO TO CHURCH, IT GIVES ME DYSENTERY.

MARK TWAIN

Your whole life is on the other side of the glass. And there is nobody watching.

ALAN BENNETT

SHOW ME A HERO AND I'LL
WRITE YOU A TRAGEDY.

F. SCOTT FITZGERALD

It's not the tragedies that
kill us, it's the messes.

DOROTHY PARKER

I WISH PEOPLE WEREN'T SO
SET ON BEING THEMSELVES,
WHEN THAT MEANS
BEING A BASTARD.

ROBERTSON DAVIES

Happiness in intelligent people
is the rarest thing I know.

ERNEST HEMINGWAY

HELL IS OTHER PEOPLE.

JEAN-PAUL SARTRE

Life has to be given a meaning
because of the obvious fact
that it has no meaning.

HENRY MILLER

BOTH OPTIMISTS AND
PESSIMISTS CONTRIBUTE
TO SOCIETY. THE
OPTIMIST INVENTS
THE AEROPLANE,
THE PESSIMIST THE
PARACHUTE.

George Bernard Shaw

UNSEEN, IN THE BACKGROUND,
FATE WAS QUIETLY
SLIPPING THE LEAD INTO
THE BOXING-GLOVE.

P. G. WODEHOUSE

A cynic is a man who, when he smells
flowers, looks around for a coffin.

H. L. MENCKEN

IF YOU FIND THIS WORLD
BAD, YOU SHOULD SEE
SOME OF THE OTHERS.

PHILIP K. DICK

A pessimist? That's a person who has been intimately acquainted with an optimist.

ELBERT HUBBARD

NINE-TENTHS OF THE PEOPLE WERE CREATED SO YOU WOULD WANT TO BE WITH THE OTHER TENTH.

HORACE WALPOLE

Anything that happens, happens.

DOUGLAS ADAMS

SCHADENFREUDE IS
SO NUTRITIOUS.

WILL SELF

Most people would sooner die
than think; in fact, they do so.

BERTRAND RUSSELL

THE MORE I LEARN
ABOUT PEOPLE, THE
MORE I LIKE MY DOG.

MARK TWAIN

PEARLS OF
WISDOM

I always pass on good advice.
It's the only thing to do with it.
It is never any use to oneself.

OSCAR WILDE

IN UNIVERSITY THEY DON'T
TELL YOU THAT THE GREATER
PART OF THE LAW IS LEARNING
TO TOLERATE FOOLS.

DORIS LESSING

Blessed is the man who, having
nothing to say, abstains from giving
wordy evidence of the fact.

GEORGE ELIOT

WISDOM IS BETTER THAN WIT, AND IN THE LONG RUN WILL CERTAINLY HAVE THE LAUGH ON HER SIDE.

JANE AUSTEN

You know how advice is. You only want it if it agrees with what you wanted to do anyway.

JOHN STEINBECK

A LEARNING EXPERIENCE IS ONE OF THOSE THINGS THAT SAYS, 'YOU KNOW THAT THING YOU JUST DID? DON'T DO THAT.'

DOUGLAS ADAMS

One can be the master of what one does, but never of what one feels.

GUSTAVE FLAUBERT

NEVER TRY TO KEEP UP WITH THE JONESES. DRAG THEM DOWN TO YOUR LEVEL. IT'S CHEAPER.

QUENTIN CRISP

A little inaccuracy sometimes saves tons of explanation.

SAKI

I OWE MY SUCCESS TO HAVING
LISTENED RESPECTFULLY...
TO THE VERY BEST ADVICE...
AND THEN GOING AWAY AND
DOING THE EXACT OPPOSITE.

G. K. CHESTERTON

Try to be a rainbow in
someone's cloud.

MAYA ANGELOU

NEVER RUIN AN APOLOGY
WITH AN EXCUSE.

BENJAMIN FRANKLIN

Don't ever take a fence down until you know why it was put up.

ROBERT FROST

If you tell the truth, you don't have to remember anything.

MARK TWAIN

You can think clearly only
with your clothes on.

MARGARET ATWOOD

ADVICE IS A DANGEROUS
GIFT, EVEN FROM THE WISE
TO THE WISE, AND ALL
COURSES MAY RUN ILL.

J. R. R. TOLKIEN

Wisely and slow; they
stumble that run fast.

WILLIAM SHAKESPEARE

I ALWAYS ADVISE PEOPLE
NEVER TO GIVE ADVICE.

P. G. WODEHOUSE

Grown-up people do not know that
a child can give exceedingly good
advice even in the most difficult case.

FYODOR DOSTOYEVSKY

ONE OF THE SECRETS OF A
HAPPY LIFE IS CONTINUOUS
SMALL TREATS.

IRIS MURDOCH

Don't try to solve serious matters in the middle of the night.

PHILIP K. DICK

Murder is always a mistake. One should never do anything that one cannot talk about after dinner.

OSCAR WILDE

IT IS BETTER TO BE QUOTABLE THAN TO BE HONEST.

TOM STOPPARD

Nobody minds having what is too good for them.

JANE AUSTEN

THE DEVIL
AND THE
ANGEL

AN UNFORTUNATE THING
ABOUT THIS WORLD IS
THAT THE GOOD HABITS
ARE MUCH EASIER TO GIVE
UP THAN THE BAD ONES.

W. SOMERSET MAUGHAM

We ought never to do wrong
when people are looking.

MARK TWAIN

HOW LIKE HERRINGS AND
ONIONS OUR VICES ARE IN
THE MORNING AFTER WE
HAVE COMMITTED THEM.

SAMUEL TAYLOR COLERIDGE

If one sticks too rigidly to one's principles, one would hardly see anybody.

AGATHA CHRISTIE

IN MANY WALKS OF LIFE, A CONSCIENCE IS A MORE EXPENSIVE ENCUMBRANCE THAN A WIFE OR A CARRIAGE.

THOMAS DE QUINCEY

No one gossips about other people's secret virtues.

BERTRAND RUSSELL

THE CHAINS OF HABIT
ARE TOO WEAK TO BE FELT
UNTIL THEY ARE TOO
STRONG TO BE BROKEN.

SAMUEL JOHNSON

I like the English. They have the most
rigid code of immorality in the world.

MALCOLM BRADBURY

IF THERE WERE NO BAD
PEOPLE, THERE WOULD BE
NO GOOD LAWYERS.

CHARLES DICKENS

I believe in getting into hot water.
I think it keeps you clean.

G. K. CHESTERTON

COMMIT THE OLDEST SINS
THE NEWEST KIND OF WAYS.

WILLIAM SHAKESPEARE

I do not want people to be very
agreeable, as it saves me the
trouble of liking them a great deal.

JANE AUSTEN

ONE SHOULD ALWAYS BE
DRUNK... WITH WINE,
WITH POETRY,
OR WITH VIRTUE, AS
YOU CHOOSE. BUT
GET DRUNK.

Charles Baudelaire

MORAL INDIGNATION IS
JEALOUSY WITH A HALO.

H. G. WELLS

Oh, blameless people are always
the most exasperating.

GEORGE ELIOT

VICES AND VIRTUES ARE OF
A STRANGE NATURE, FOR
THE MORE WE HAVE, THE
FEWER WE THINK WE HAVE.

ALEXANDER POPE

In England the only homage which
they pay to Virtue – is hypocrisy.

LORD BYRON

A VICE IS ONLY AN
EXAGGERATION OF
A NECESSARY AND
VIRTUOUS FUNCTION.

RALPH WALDO EMERSON

The lack of money is
the root of all evil.

MARK TWAIN

ALL THE MOTIVES FOR
MURDER ARE COVERED
BY FOUR Ls: LOVE, LUST,
LUCRE AND LOATHING.

P. D. JAMES

It is good to be without vices, but it is
not good to be without temptations.

WALTER BAGEHOT

THE FIXITY OF A HABIT
IS GENERALLY IN
DIRECT PROPORTION
TO ITS ABSURDITY.

MARCEL PROUST

The best cure for one's bad
tendencies is to see them in
action in another person.

ALAIN DE BOTTON

GOOD AND BAD MEN
ARE EACH LESS SO
THAN THEY SEEM.

SAMUEL TAYLOR COLERIDGE

Some rise by sin, and
some by virtue fall.

WILLIAM SHAKESPEARE

AMORE
AND MORE

LOVE IS AN IRRESISTIBLE DESIRE TO BE IRRESISTIBLY DESIRED.

ROBERT FROST

Sex is one of the nine reasons
for reincarnation. The other
eight are unimportant.

HENRY MILLER

LOVE IS WHAT HAPPENS TO A MAN AND WOMAN WHO DON'T KNOW EACH OTHER.

W. SOMERSET MAUGHAM

There is no remedy for
love but to love more.

HENRY DAVID THOREAU

IT WAS LOVE AT FIRST
SIGHT, AT LAST SIGHT, AT
EVER AND EVER SIGHT.

VLADIMIR NABOKOV

Sex is kicking death in the
ass while singing.

CHARLES BUKOWSKI

IN LOVE, ONE AND ONE ARE ONE.

JEAN-PAUL SARTRE

Let us forget with generosity those who cannot love us.

PABLO NERUDA

TO FEAR LOVE IS TO FEAR LIFE, AND THOSE WHO FEAR LIFE ARE ALREADY THREE PARTS DEAD.

BERTRAND RUSSELL

Every man needs two women: a quiet home-maker, and a thrilling nymph.

IRIS MURDOCH

Who so loves believes the impossible.

ELIZABETH BARRETT BROWNING

Sex without love is as hollow and
ridiculous as love without sex.

HUNTER S. THOMPSON

A HISTORICAL ROMANCE
IS THE ONLY KIND OF
BOOK WHERE CHASTITY
REALLY COUNTS.

BARBARA CARTLAND

Only the united beat of sex and
heart together can create ecstasy.

ANAÏS NIN

YOU MUSTN'T FORCE SEX TO
DO THE WORK OF LOVE OR
LOVE TO DO THE WORK OF SEX.

MARY McCARTHY

To love and win is the best thing.
To love and lose, the next best.

WILLIAM MAKEPEACE THACKERAY

IT IS DIFFICULT TO KNOW
AT WHAT MOMENT LOVE
BEGINS; IT IS LESS DIFFICULT TO
KNOW THAT IT HAS BEGUN.

HENRY WADSWORTH LONGFELLOW

Were kisses all the joys in bed,
One woman would another wed.

WILLIAM SHAKESPEARE

I WRITE ABOUT SEX
BECAUSE OFTEN IT FEELS
LIKE THE MOST IMPORTANT
THING IN THE WORLD.

JEANETTE WINTERSON

What holds the world together,
as I have learned from bitter
experience, is sexual intercourse.

HENRY MILLER

There are all kinds of love in this world, but never the same love twice.

F. SCOTT FITZGERALD

LOVE HAS NO UTTERMOST, AS
THE STARS HAVE NO NUMBER
AND THE SEA NO REST.

ELEANOR FARJEON

Licence my roving hands,
and let them go,
Before, behind, between,
above, below.

JOHN DONNE

MARITAL

HISS

ADVICE TO PERSONS ABOUT TO MARRY – DON'T.

HENRY MAYHEW

One should always be in love. That is the reason one should never marry.

OSCAR WILDE

THERE ARE MEN WHO FEAR REPARTEE IN A WIFE MORE KEENLY THAN A SWORD.

P. G. WODEHOUSE

The triumph of hope
over experience.

SAMUEL JOHNSON ON SECOND MARRIAGES

IF A WOMAN DOUBTS
AS TO WHETHER SHE
SHOULD ACCEPT A MAN
OR NOT, SHE CERTAINLY
OUGHT TO REFUSE HIM.

JANE AUSTEN

Wishing each other, not
divorced, but dead;
They lived respectably
as man and wife.

LORD BYRON

The tragedy is when you've
got sex in the head instead
of down where it belongs.

D. H. LAWRENCE

LAUGH AND THE WORLD
LAUGHS WITH YOU; SNORE
AND YOU SLEEP ALONE.

ANTHONY BURGESS

I have always thought that every
woman should marry, and no man.

BENJAMIN DISRAELI

WHAT GOD HATH JOINED
TOGETHER NO MAN EVER
SHALL PUT ASUNDER: GOD
WILL TAKE CARE OF THAT.

GEORGE BERNARD SHAW

The most happy marriage I can
picture or imagine to myself
would be the union of a deaf
man to a blind woman.

SAMUEL TAYLOR COLERIDGE

HOLY DEADLOCK

**THE TITLE OF A. P. HERBERT'S SATIRICAL
NOVEL ON DIVORCE LAW**

ONE DOESN'T HAVE TO
GET ANYWHERE IN A
MARRIAGE. IT'S NOT A
PUBLIC CONVEYANCE.

Iris Murdoch

'Suffer the little children to come unto me.' You might know Jesus wasn't married.

ALAN BENNETT

MARRIAGE MAY OFTEN
BE A STORMY LAKE, BUT
CELIBACY IS ALMOST ALWAYS
A MUDDY HORSEPOND.

THOMAS LOVE PEACOCK

Bachelors know more about women than married men. If they did not they would be married too.

H. L. MENCKEN

STRANGE TO SAY WHAT
DELIGHT WE MARRIED
PEOPLE HAVE TO SEE THESE
POOR FOOLS DECOYED
INTO OUR CONDITION.

SAMUEL PEPYS

Marriage is a feast where the grace
is sometimes better than the dinner.

CHARLES CALEB COLTON

CHUMPS ALWAYS MAKE
THE BEST HUSBANDS... ALL
THE UNHAPPY MARRIAGES
COME FROM THE HUSBANDS
HAVING BRAINS.

P. G. WODEHOUSE

DEDICATED

FOLLOWERS

OF FASHION

Clothes make the man.
Naked people have little or
no influence on society.

MARK TWAIN

HIS SOCKS COMPELLED
ONE'S ATTENTION WITHOUT
LOSING ONE'S RESPECT.

SAKI

A fine coat is a livery, when the
person who wears it discovers no
higher sense than that of a footman.

JOSEPH ADDISON

IF A WOMAN REBELS AGAINST
HIGH-HEELED SHOES, SHE
SHOULD TAKE CARE TO DO
IT IN A VERY SMART HAT.

GEORGE BERNARD SHAW

A well-tied tie is the first
serious step in life.

OSCAR WILDE

OH, NEVER MIND THE
FASHION. WHEN ONE HAS A
STYLE OF ONE'S OWN, IT IS
ALWAYS 20 TIMES BETTER.

MARGARET OLIPHANT

Every generation laughs at
the old fashions, but follows
religiously the new.

HENRY DAVID THOREAU

THERE IS ONE OTHER REASON
FOR DRESSING WELL...
NAMELY, THAT DOGS RESPECT
IT, AND WILL NOT ATTACK
YOU IN GOOD CLOTHES.

RALPH WALDO EMERSON

Where's the man could ease a heart
Like a satin gown?

DOROTHY PARKER

FASHION IS WHAT YOU
ADOPT WHEN YOU DON'T
KNOW WHO YOU ARE.

QUENTIN CRISP

Fine clothes may disguise, but
silly words will disclose a fool.

AESOP

MISTRUST ALL ENTERPRISES
THAT REQUIRE NEW CLOTHES.

E. M. FORSTER

Vain trifles as they seem, clothes... change our view of the world and the world's view of us.

VIRGINIA WOOLF

Perfect simplicity is unconsciously audacious.

GEORGE MEREDITH

It's wisest always to be so clad that our friends need not ask us for our names.

JAMES FENIMORE COOPER

SHE DID WHAT GIRLS GENERALLY DO WHEN THEY DON'T FEEL THE PART: SHE DRESSED IT INSTEAD.

ZADIE SMITH

Style is knowing who you are, what you want to say, and not giving a damn.

GORE VIDAL

THE BOOR COVERS HIMSELF,
THE RICH MAN OR THE FOOL
ADORNS HIMSELF, AND THE
ELEGANT MAN GETS DRESSED.

HONORÉ DE BALZAC

One should either be a work of
art, or wear a work of art.

OSCAR WILDE

FASHION IS GENTILITY
RUNNING AWAY FROM
VULGARITY, AND AFRAID OF
BEING OVERTAKEN BY IT.

WILLIAM HAZLITT

After all, those fine clothes were once worn by a sheep, and they never turned it into anything better than a sheep.

THOMAS MORE

A QUOTABLE
FEAST

If more of us valued food and cheer and song above hoarded gold, it would be a merrier world.

J. R. R. TOLKIEN

THERE IS NO LOVE SINCERER THAN THE LOVE OF FOOD.

GEORGE BERNARD SHAW

Eating and reading are two pleasures that combine admirably.

C. S. LEWIS

GOOD APPLE PIES ARE A
CONSIDERABLE PART OF
OUR DOMESTIC HAPPINESS.

JANE AUSTEN

No animal ever invented
anything so bad as drunkenness
– or so good as drink.

G. K. CHESTERTON

A TAVERN IS A PLACE
WHERE MADNESS IS SOLD
BY THE BOTTLE.

JONATHAN SWIFT

Coffee in England always tastes
like a chemistry experiment.

AGATHA CHRISTIE

ONE CANNOT THINK WELL,
LOVE WELL, SLEEP WELL, IF
ONE HAS NOT DINED WELL.

VIRGINIA WOOLF

After a full belly all is poetry.

FRANK McCOURT

TO EAT WELL IN ENGLAND
YOU SHOULD HAVE BREAKFAST
THREE TIMES A DAY.

W. SOMERSET MAUGHAM

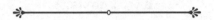

What I say is that, if a man really
likes potatoes, he must be a
pretty decent sort of fellow.

A. A. MILNE

PART OF THE SECRET OF
SUCCESS IN LIFE IS TO EAT
WHAT YOU LIKE AND LET THE
FOOD FIGHT IT OUT INSIDE.

MARK TWAIN

We must have a pie. Stress cannot
exist in the presence of a pie.

DAVID MAMET

THERE IS ONE THING MORE
EXASPERATING THAN A WIFE
WHO CAN COOK AND WON'T,
AND THAT'S A WIFE WHO
CAN'T COOK AND WILL.

ROBERT FROST

Music with dinner is an insult both
to the cook and the violinist.

G. K. CHESTERTON

NO MAN IS LONELY WHILE EATING SPAGHETTI: IT REQUIRES SO MUCH ATTENTION.

Christopher Morley

HE WAS A BOLD MAN THAT
FIRST ATE AN OYSTER.

JONATHAN SWIFT

All sorrows are less with bread.

MIGUEL DE CERVANTES

ALCOHOL MAKES OTHER
PEOPLE LESS TEDIOUS... AND
CAN HELP PROVIDE... THE
SLIGHT BUZZ OF INSPIRATION
WHEN READING OR WRITING.

CHRISTOPHER HITCHENS

Mayonnaise… one of the
sauces which serve the French
in place of a state religion.

AMBROSE BIERCE

THERE ARE ONLY TEN MINUTES
IN THE LIFE OF A PEAR WHEN
IT IS PERFECT TO EAT.

RALPH WALDO EMERSON

I think it could be plausibly
argued that changes of diet are
more important than changes
of dynasty or… religion.

GEORGE ORWELL

MADAM, I HAVE BEEN LOOKING
FOR A PERSON WHO DISLIKED
GRAVY ALL MY LIFE; LET US
SWEAR ETERNAL FRIENDSHIP.

SYDNEY SMITH

I hate people who are not serious
about meals. It is so shallow of them.

OSCAR WILDE

THE CURSE
OF THE
DRINKING
CLASSES

IT IS IMPOSSIBLE TO ENJOY
IDLING THOROUGHLY
UNLESS ONE HAS PLENTY
OF WORK TO DO.

JEROME K. JEROME

The best way to appreciate your job
is to imagine yourself without one.

OSCAR WILDE

ONE OF THE SYMPTOMS OF
AN APPROACHING NERVOUS
BREAKDOWN IS THE BELIEF
THAT ONE'S WORK IS
TERRIBLY IMPORTANT.

BERTRAND RUSSELL

Term, holidays, term, holidays,
till we leave school, and then
work, work, work till we die.

C. S. LEWIS

THERE'S NO MONEY IN
POETRY, BUT THEN THERE'S NO
POETRY IN MONEY, EITHER.

ROBERT GRAVES

One forges one's style on the
terrible anvil of daily deadlines.

ÉMILE ZOLA

NOTHING IS REALLY WORK
UNLESS YOU WOULD RATHER
BE DOING SOMETHING ELSE.

J. M. BARRIE

I love deadlines. I love the whooshing
noise they make as they go by.

DOUGLAS ADAMS

SET ME ANYTHING TO
DO AS A TASK, AND IT IS
INCONCEIVABLE THE DESIRE I
HAVE TO DO SOMETHING ELSE.

GEORGE BERNARD SHAW

It's the job that's never started as takes longest to finish.

J. R. R. TOLKIEN

If at first you don't succeed, failure may be your style.

QUENTIN CRISP

A man is not idle, because
he is absorbed in thought.
There is a visible labour and
there is an invisible labour.

VICTOR HUGO

THERE IS NO SUCH THING
AS WORK–LIFE BALANCE.
EVERYTHING WORTH FIGHTING
FOR UNBALANCES YOUR LIFE.

ALAIN DE BOTTON

Hard work is a prison sentence
only if it does not have meaning.

MALCOLM GLADWELL

ANY DAMN FOOL CAN BEG
UP SOME KIND OF JOB; IT
TAKES A WISE MAN TO MAKE
IT WITHOUT WORKING.

CHARLES BUKOWSKI

Hard work should be
rewarded by good food.

KEN FOLLETT

HOW LITTLE OUR CAREERS
EXPRESS WHAT LIES IN US, AND
YET HOW MUCH TIME THEY
TAKE UP. IT'S SAD, REALLY.

PHILIP LARKIN

A large income is the best recipe for happiness I ever heard of.

JANE AUSTEN

Every acquisition that is
disproportionate to the labour
spent on it is dishonest.

LEO TOLSTOY

TO DO GREAT WORK A MAN
MUST BE VERY IDLE AS WELL
AS VERY INDUSTRIOUS.

SAMUEL BUTLER

THIS
SPORTING
LIFE

There are only three sports:
bullfighting, motor racing,
and mountaineering; all the
rest are merely games.

ERNEST HEMINGWAY

GOLF IS A GAME IN WHICH
YOU CAN CLAIM THE
PRIVILEGES OF AGE AND
RETAIN THE PLAYTHINGS
OF CHILDHOOD.

SAMUEL JOHNSON

If all the year were playing holidays,
To sport would be as tedious as to work.

WILLIAM SHAKESPEARE

RUGBY IS A GOOD
OCCASION FOR KEEPING
30 BULLIES FAR FROM THE
CENTRE OF THE CITY.

OSCAR WILDE

Deer-stalking would be a very fine
sport if only the deer had guns.

W. S. GILBERT

BASEBALL HAS THE GREAT
ADVANTAGE OVER CRICKET
OF BEING SOONER ENDED.

GEORGE BERNARD SHAW

I bowl so slow that if after I
have delivered the ball I don't
like the look of it, I can run
after it and bring it back.

J. M. BARRIE ON CRICKET

SUDDEN SUCCESS IN GOLF
IS LIKE THE SUDDEN
ACQUISITION OF WEALTH.
IT IS APT TO UNSETTLE AND
DETERIORATE THE CHARACTER.

P. G. WODEHOUSE

I once jogged to the ashtray.

WILL SELF ON HIS SPORTING HABITS

I MUST COMPLAIN THE CARDS ARE ILL SHUFFLED, TILL I HAVE A GOOD HAND.

JONATHAN SWIFT

It is foolish and quite unfitting for an educated man to spend all his time on acquiring bulging muscles, a thick neck and mighty thighs. The large amounts they are compelled to eat make them dull-witted.

SENECA

I NEVER DID LIKE WORKING OUT – IT BEARS THE SAME RELATIONSHIP TO REAL SPORT AS MASTURBATION DOES TO REAL SEX.

DAVID LODGE

GOLF IS A DAY SPENT IN A ROUND OF STRENUOUS IDLENESS.

William Wordsworth

Serious sport has nothing
to do with fair play… It is
war minus the shooting.

GEORGE ORWELL

IF YOU THINK SQUASH IS A
COMPETITIVE ACTIVITY, TRY
FLOWER ARRANGEMENT.

ALAN BENNETT

The thing about football – the
important thing about football – is
that it is not just about football.

TERRY PRATCHETT

DEFEATED MISERY IS WHAT ALL
SPORT IS ABOUT, EVENTUALLY,
IF YOU FOLLOW THE STORY
FOR LONG ENOUGH.

NICK HORNBY

The profession of book writing
makes horse racing seem like
a solid, stable business.

JOHN STEINBECK

THE FASCINATION OF
SHOOTING AS A SPORT
DEPENDS ALMOST WHOLLY
ON WHETHER YOU ARE
AT THE RIGHT OR WRONG
END OF THE GUN.

P. G. WODEHOUSE

Of course I have played outdoor
games. I once played dominoes
in an open-air cafe in Paris.

OSCAR WILDE

WHAT EXACTLY *DO* I THINK
ABOUT WHEN I'M RUNNING?
I DON'T HAVE A CLUE.

HARUKI MURAKAMI

The only athletic sport I ever
mastered was backgammon.

DOUGLAS JERROLD

IN THE
STICKS OR
THE CITY

GOD MADE THE COUNTRY,
AND MAN MADE THE TOWN.

WILLIAM COWPER

I have never understood why
anybody agreed to go on being
a rustic after about 1400.

KINGSLEY AMIS

PARIS IS A WOMAN
BUT LONDON IS AN
INDEPENDENT MAN PUFFING
HIS PIPE IN A PUB.

JACK KEROUAC

Anyone can be good in the country.
There are no temptations there.

OSCAR WILDE

IN LONDON, MAN IS THE MOST
SECRET ANIMAL ON EARTH.

LAURIE LEE

When I am in the country I wish
to vegetate like the country.

WILLIAM HAZLITT

MY LIVING IN YORKSHIRE
WAS SO FAR OUT OF THE WAY,
THAT IT WAS ACTUALLY 12
MILES FROM A LEMON.

SYDNEY SMITH

No city should be too large for a
man to walk out of in a morning.

CYRIL CONNOLLY

A SMALL COUNTRY TOWN IS
NOT THE PLACE IN WHICH ONE
WOULD CHOOSE TO QUARREL
WITH A WIFE; EVERY HUMAN
BEING IN SUCH PLACES IS A SPY.

SAMUEL JOHNSON

City life is millions of people being lonesome together.

HENRY DAVID THOREAU

A large city cannot be experientially known; its life is too manifold for any individual to be able to participate in it.

ALDOUS HUXLEY

The city is recruited from
the country.

RALPH WALDO EMERSON

THE LOWEST AND VILEST
ALLEYS IN LONDON DO NOT
PRESENT A MORE DREADFUL
RECORD OF SIN THAN
DOES THE SMILING AND
BEAUTIFUL COUNTRYSIDE.

ARTHUR CONAN DOYLE

We do not look in great cities
for our best morality.

JANE AUSTEN

A GREAT CITY IS THAT WHICH HAS THE GREATEST MEN AND WOMEN.

WALT WHITMAN

I suppose the pleasure of country life lies really in the eternally renewed evidences of the determination to live.

VITA SACKVILLE-WEST

I HAVE NO RELISH FOR THE COUNTRY; IT IS A KIND OF HEALTHY GRAVE.

SYDNEY SMITH

In my time, the follies of the town crept slowly among us, but now they travel faster than a stage-coach.

OLIVER GOLDSMITH

London is a riddle. Paris
is an explanation.

G. K. CHESTERTON

JUST LIVING IS NOT
ENOUGH... ONE MUST
HAVE SUNSHINE, FREEDOM,
AND A LITTLE FLOWER.

HANS CHRISTIAN ANDERSEN

SCIENTIFICALLY
LITERATE

Everything starts somewhere,
although many physicists disagree.

TERRY PRATCHETT

READING COMPUTER MANUALS
WITHOUT THE HARDWARE
IS AS FRUSTRATING AS
READING SEX MANUALS
WITHOUT THE SOFTWARE.

ARTHUR C. CLARKE

Technological progress has merely
provided us with more efficient
means for going backwards.

ALDOUS HUXLEY

SCIENCE NEVER SOLVES
A PROBLEM WITHOUT
CREATING TEN MORE.

GEORGE BERNARD SHAW

Invention, in my opinion,
arises directly from idleness,
possibly also from laziness –
to save oneself trouble.

AGATHA CHRISTIE

ONE MACHINE CAN DO THE
WORK OF 50 ORDINARY
MEN. NO MACHINE CAN
DO THE WORK OF ONE
EXTRAORDINARY MAN.

ELBERT HUBBARD

Don't explain computers to laymen.
Simpler to explain sex to a virgin.

ROBERT A. HEINLEIN

BOOKS DON'T
NEED BATTERIES.

NADINE GORDIMER

We are stuck with technology
when what we really want
is just stuff that works.

DOUGLAS ADAMS

INVENTOR...
A PERSON WHO
MAKES AN INGENIOUS
ARRANGEMENT OF
WHEELS, LEVERS AND
SPRINGS, AND BELIEVES
IT CIVILISATION.

Ambrose Bierce

TECHNOLOGY PRESUMES
THERE'S JUST ONE RIGHT
WAY TO DO THINGS
AND THERE NEVER IS.

ROBERT M. PIRSIG

Men have become the
tools of their tools.

HENRY DAVID THOREAU

COMPUTERS ARE LIKE OLD
TESTAMENT GODS; LOTS OF
RULES AND NO MERCY.

JOSEPH CAMPBELL

The saddest aspect of life right now
is that science gathers knowledge
faster than society gathers wisdom.

ISAAC ASIMOV

THAT WHICH CAN BE ASSERTED
WITHOUT EVIDENCE, CAN BE
DISMISSED WITHOUT EVIDENCE.

CHRISTOPHER HITCHENS

We are an impossibility in
an impossible universe.

RAY BRADBURY

INVENTION, IT MUST BE HUMBLY ADMITTED, DOES NOT CONSIST OF CREATING OUT OF VOID, BUT OUT OF CHAOS.

MARY SHELLEY

I like the scientific spirit – the holding off, the being sure but not too sure, the willingness to surrender ideas when the evidence is against them.

WALT WHITMAN

ANY SUFFICIENTLY ADVANCED TECHNOLOGY IS INDISTINGUISHABLE FROM MAGIC.

ARTHUR C. CLARKE

MORE THINGS IN HEAVEN AND EARTH....

It is the test of a good religion
whether you can joke about it.

G. K. CHESTERTON

THE PURITAN HATED BEAR-
BAITING, NOT BECAUSE IT
GAVE PAIN TO THE BEAR, BUT
BECAUSE IT GAVE PLEASURE
TO THE SPECTATORS.

THOMAS BABINGTON MACAULAY

To a philosophic eye, the
vices of the clergy are far less
dangerous than their virtues.

EDWARD GIBBON

HERESY IS ONLY ANOTHER WORD FOR FREEDOM OF THOUGHT.

GRAHAM GREENE

It may be that our role on this planet is not to worship God but to create him.

ARTHUR C. CLARKE

AS THE FRENCH SAY, THERE ARE THREE SEXES – MEN, WOMEN AND CLERGYMEN.

SYDNEY SMITH

We have not lost faith, but we
have transferred it from God
to the medical profession.

GEORGE BERNARD SHAW

FOR WHAT A MAN WOULD
LIKE TO BE TRUE, THAT HE
MORE READILY BELIEVES.

FRANCIS BACON

The New Testament is basically
about what happened
when God got religion.

TERRY PRATCHETT

I cannot believe in a God who wants to be praised all the time.

FRIEDRICH NIETZSCHE

The easy confidence with which I know another man's religion is folly teaches me to suspect that my own is also.

MARK TWAIN

PROPERLY READ, THE BIBLE IS THE MOST POTENT FORCE FOR ATHEISM EVER CONCEIVED.

ISAAC ASIMOV

Do not wait for the last judgement. It comes every day.

ALBERT CAMUS

FROM THE BEGINNING MEN USED GOD TO JUSTIFY THE UNJUSTIFIABLE.

SALMAN RUSHDIE

One good schoolmaster is of more use than 100 priests.

THOMAS PAINE

REALITY PROVIDES US WITH FACTS SO ROMANTIC THAT IMAGINATION ITSELF COULD ADD NOTHING TO THEM.

JULES VERNE

When we blindly adopt a religion, a political system, a literary dogma, we become automatons. We cease to grow.

ANAÏS NIN

I AM A RELIGIOUS
PERSON, ALTHOUGH I
AM NOT A BELIEVER.

PHILIP PULLMAN

You can't teach an old
dogma new tricks.

DOROTHY PARKER

THE DEVIL CAN CITE
SCRIPTURE FOR HIS PURPOSE.

WILLIAM SHAKESPEARE

FOR THE
LOVE OF
BOOKS

One always tends to overpraise
a long book, because one
has got through it.

E. M. FORSTER

DEFINITION OF A CLASSIC: A
BOOK EVERYONE IS ASSUMED
TO HAVE READ AND OFTEN
THINKS THEY HAVE.

ALAN BENNETT

The only demand I make of my
reader is that he should devote his
whole life to reading my works.

JAMES JOYCE

NO PLACE AFFORDS A MORE
STRIKING CONVICTION OF THE
VANITY OF HUMAN HOPES,
THAN A PUBLIC LIBRARY.

SAMUEL JOHNSON

When I want to read a
novel, I write one.

BENJAMIN DISRAELI

A MAN CAN NEVER HAVE
TOO MUCH RED WINE, TOO
MANY BOOKS, OR TOO
MUCH AMMUNITION.

RUDYARD KIPLING

The remarkable thing about
Shakespeare is that he really
is very good, in spite of all the
people who say he is very good.

ROBERT GRAVES

THE PERSON, BE IT GENTLEMAN
OR LADY, WHO HAS NOT
PLEASURE IN A GOOD NOVEL,
MUST BE INTOLERABLY STUPID.

JANE AUSTEN

No human being ever spoke of
scenery for above two minutes at a
time, which makes me suspect that
we hear too much of it in literature.

ROBERT LOUIS STEVENSON

IT IS WHAT YOU READ WHEN
YOU DON'T HAVE TO THAT
DETERMINES WHAT YOU WILL
BE WHEN YOU CAN'T HELP IT.

OSCAR WILDE

There are two motives for reading
a book: one, that you enjoy it; the
other, that you can boast about it.

BERTRAND RUSSELL

ONE HATES AN AUTHOR
THAT'S ALL AUTHOR.

LORD BYRON

For most of my reading I go back
to the old ones – for comfort.

DOROTHY PARKER

A BOOK IS A MIRROR: IF
AN ASS PEERS INTO IT,
YOU CAN'T EXPECT AN
APOSTLE TO LOOK OUT.

GEORG CHRISTOPH LICHTENBERG

Do not read, as children do, to
amuse yourself, or like the ambitious,
for the purpose of instruction.
No, read in order to live.

GUSTAVE FLAUBERT

WHEN I GET A LITTLE
MONEY, I BUY BOOKS;
AND IF ANY IS LEFT, I BUY
FOOD AND CLOTHES.

DESIDERIUS ERASMUS

Reading is not a duty, and has
consequently no business to
be made disagreeable.

AUGUSTINE BIRRELL

A BOOK IS A FRAGILE
CREATURE, IT SUFFERS THE
WEAR OF TIME, IT FEARS
RODENTS, THE ELEMENTS,
CLUMSY HANDS.

UMBERTO ECO

I would sooner read a timetable or a catalogue than nothing at all.

W. SOMERSET MAUGHAM

Fiction is like a spider's web, attached ever so lightly perhaps, but still attached to life at all four corners.

VIRGINIA WOOLF

He who lends a book is an
idiot. He who returns the
book is more of an idiot.

ARABIC PROVERB

BORROWERS OF BOOKS –
THOSE MUTILATORS OF
COLLECTIONS, SPOILERS OF THE
SYMMETRY OF SHELVES, AND
CREATORS OF ODD VOLUMES.

CHARLES LAMB

Having to read a footnote
resembles having to go downstairs
to answer the door while in
the midst of making love.

NOËL COWARD

READING IS LIKE PERMITTING
A MAN TO TALK A LONG
TIME, AND REFUSING YOU
THE RIGHT TO ANSWER.

EDGAR WATSON HOWE

A writer only begins a book.
A reader finishes it.

SAMUEL JOHNSON

IF BOOKS ARE NOT
GOOD COMPANY, WHERE
WILL I FIND IT?

MARK TWAIN

SOME BOOKS ARE TO BE TASTED, OTHERS TO BE SWALLOWED, AND SOME FEW TO BE CHEWED AND DIGESTED; THAT IS, SOME BOOKS ARE TO BE READ ONLY IN PARTS; OTHERS TO BE READ, BUT NOT CURIOUSLY; AND SOME FEW TO BE READ WHOLLY, AND WITH DILIGENCE AND ATTENTION.

Francis Bacon

If you're interested in finding out more about our books, find us on Facebook at **Summersdale Publishers** and follow us on Twitter at **@Summersdale**.

www.summersdale.com